Feed.

a collection of poetry

By Sarah Marie Vetter

Copyright © 2020 by Sarah Marie Vetter
All rights reserved.

Forward

What is it trying to show you...
If you can see it, then you can use it.
If you can use it, then it is a source of fuel.
Your next source to harness and propel you forward.

My intention is to share everything I've felt and have experienced in my darks, relationships, and in finding and growing my light. The things that have given me strength and helped me grow. Years of lessons from my mistakes in the hopes that some of these may help you along your way.

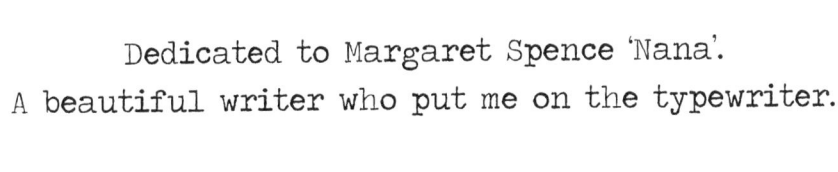

Dedicated to Margaret Spence 'Nana'.
A beautiful writer who put me on the typewriter.

Contents

Ground 1

Affirm 17

Love 33

Light 53

Ground

For You

For you to pause,
For you to empty the cluttered drawers of
your house and mind.

For you to paint and dance and
sleep in the mid afternoon,
after a walk in the quiet rain.

For you to connect.
For you to disconnect.

For you to nest.
For you to rest.

It's all for you.

The Most Beautiful Spots

The most beautiful spots, where the roots take hold.

Are deep within the dark muck and space of an undirected soul.

This space where you can't discern up from down, deep in the dark lands where you search for solid ground.

Grabbing at the dirt you find some godforsaken way to navigate a new route.

Mixing the surrounding earth until you find strength to assimilate to.

These, only in hindsight, are the most beautiful spaces you pass through. Rich with growth, solid in yourself alone- creatively rebuilding the unique earth that surrounds you.

In The Dark

It's dark down there
There's not much air
Damp, small and smokey.

Some part of you still believes you're not worthy
and lovable.

You don't need that darkness anymore.
It's not true, has never been true or will ever
be true. The only truth is you are love.
Fully and wholly,
Sparkling atoms of love.

Goodnight

I had a dream I put you to sleep.

You were tired, and sad, but beautifully unfulfilled and naive in your party dress.

You closed your eyes and I kissed you goodnight.

I told you I loved you and you did your very best.
Then you smiled, eyes closed, content, free to rest.

I looked back once as I opened the door, sympathetic and full hearted with no regrets.
I closed the door walking into the light and leaving you to rest.

Sliver

The light came in as quietly as the darkness.
As if to calm and cautiously comfort.

Subtly I met it with question.
The dark was home, from surrendering to its presence.

Consistently it shone beckoning attention. Flirting with my eyes then brightening from my affection.

Baby Steps

Baby steps, baby steps.
Pitter patter into what life
Brings next.

No need to run- avoid the stumble.

Slow-steady-conscious
Welcoming
And
Humble.

Unpack

Unpack from day 1
The small impressionable moments, and the bigger ones.

Unpack them with love and compassion.
With understanding for every soul's role.

We all get a bag- the contents are the gift
not the burden.

Don't underestimate the task-
It is a long and arduous journey.

But the most humble, empowering march toward
unconditional love, the source of happiness and
fulfillment we are all in search of.

Everything You've Been Missing

Why do you step out instead of in?

I watch them grasp for security and validation in empty spaces that will never fulfill them.

You already have the answers and strength- but you distract yourself from depositing and withdrawing from your own bank.

How long will you do the same and expect different- before you sit and witness the energy in you to manifest everything you've been missing…

You keep forgetting

You keep forgetting, your skin is like light on snow, you make everything around you glow.

You keep forgetting, your heart is compassionate beyond measure.

Your totally magically unique talents capture.

The space you hold for old souls and new. You are an unforgettable beauty.

Don't lose your sight looking out- hold your circle of light and honor yourself.

Yin

More yin, gentle
More yin, peace
More yin, love
More yin, your gentle
More yin, your peace

More yin
My
Love.

The Key

That space in between,
Where you think lonely lives.
That's where you are.

Those fears don't exist-
Invisible chains you've strapped on.

Recognize your strength,
It will release you.

Unbind the tethers you've uncomfortably strapped
yourself to.

Your strength will become your wings delivering
you from the weight that bound you.
You alone possess the keys
To
Free
You.

Settle

Settle in.
Settle into your quiet.
slumbering depths and soul floor.

Let the comfortable- be comfortable.

Calm can be disturbing in our endlessly moving world
Drop in.
Settle in.

Welcome the calm,
Nuzzle it- get acquainted

Let
Yourself
Stay
There.

Remember

Don't hide.
You are safe here.
You belong, precious one.
Do not be afraid.
Remember.

Equilibrium

I don't want to chase anything,
I don't have the energy.

My energy will go into balancing my body,
work and relationships.
Bringing me to a harmonizing,
Radiating equilibrium of my body and soul.
Causing my true desires to attract to me,
And my life to effortlessly flow.

Affirm

Opinion Nation

Degrees of separation. When one is growing and the others speak with a tone of negative frustration.

But do you see what that soul has taken? Where their choice and path has led them?

Judgement comes from a place of disassociation, where you're either unaware or see your own limitations.

So unless you are in the ring fighting your own reflection, your opinion on their growth is without foundation.

Keep fanning your light, you are your only competition.

Bloom

You got this. You got you.

You make the sparkles,
Hold the key,
Spark the flame.

Just keep coming back to you boo,
And all that makes you bright and bloom.

Surf

In, under, through, over
To a year of smooth, intrinsic, essential behavior.

Your bones, blood, and muscles will ping you to which waves to take.

Keep following the chill-flowing-love filled vibes to unfold all your catered surprises and solidify your now deeply acknowledged worth.

She settled.

Into the space she made,
Into the energy she held,
Into the world she created for herself.

Each moment became the duvet
She had quilted and wrapped around her.

Warm, light and held.
Every stitch she warily had sewn,
She now saw and revelled as whole.

She Broke

She broke the rules
She broke the mold

She left their beliefs challenged
And their hearts full

She opened them
Breaking them open to a whole new world.

It's Always There

It's always there,
The stars twinkling between your eyes.
The expansive, endless wonder of what is right in
front of you and what is right around the next corner.

This is your dream.
Enrich your eyes.

Under You

This here is the foundation.
The concrete your angels mixed with you.

Blended, poured, leveled.

Carefully. Strategically. Intentionally.

Stand on it now,
Firmly it holds the truth of your mistakes
and triumphs.

Under you. For you.

To hold and guide you for all that is ahead of you.

Holding Space

Where the silence was empty and loud,
Stillness alone now charged me core to crown.

Where my mind's home was like a fare park swing,
Up and down in circles of experiences,
Spinning.

Now sat firmly the bench of oak rich lessons,
supporting and willing my presence.
Holding space to awe the view of life's permeable effervescence.

Uncovered

I feel myself prying myself open.

When I catch my resistance, I force myself to breathe into.

Breathe through the walls so there is a way through.

Slowly feeling safe to be uncovered by you.

In Love

She fell deeply in love with the way she opened her
eyes to the day,
The way she drank her coffee and applied
her lip stain.

She fell hard for the rhythm of her day, the things
that changed and the routines that stayed the same.

The magic hour, bedtime stories and the night that
calmed her soul and brain.

She became infatuated by the moments in between and
the hello's of new and old faces made her beam.

She found grace in experiencing her day, as if it
were new when it was all the same.

Keep

Keep the quiet confident stillness within me, let me hone it and grow it until it envelops me. Full of love and grace have my energy surround me - protect me, and heal that which needs to be set free.

Softly

Softly I follow the angles of my face.

Softly I wash the strength of my heart.

Softly I stand on my foundation.

Softly I love. Softly I live.

The Journey

If you are brutally honest and curious on your
journey, like a soldier you pave the way for many.

So get better at rescuing yourself back up, don't use
your fall to coddle negativity in the rough.

Take the lesson, and jump back up,
Because you are someone else's hero carving
the way to triumph.

The Path

When you cut out the noise.

Set the boundaries.

The path is so much wider and clearer.

Tiptoes turn into strides with sparks and light inside.

Love

Athlete of Love

Each time she was faster.
Faster at feeling,
Faster at falling,
Faster at finding her feet and strength again,
When she would lose it briefly.

She was becoming an athlete of love.

Whispers

He crept in quietly,
As though he didn't want me to see.

He whispered his way around me-
As if to take in every aspect of my energy.

He looked at me knowingly with eyes that said
"Hello again"

He reached out his hand- and when we touched, I quietly opened to his whispering, and let him in.

The Guide

A gaze that can't benchmark time,
And penetrates your truth.

If you are blessed with a loyal angel whose eyes are home to you.

Their lessons in love will change the judgements that have unconsciously blinded and misguided you.

They reflect your enduring love and compassion. Our truth we at times lose along the path to our souls exactitude.

The reason they leave this earth before me and you, is they already live in the state we live to grow to.

Present in love each moment to its deepest truth.
Love and gratitude for the present moment a gifted state we aspire to.

Boundaries

She was too young to do it then,
Didn't know her voice could protect her heart
from them.

Now that she has found the seat of her soul,
She is strong enough to let everyone know.
These are the places you cannot go,
For us to grow in love and let peace prevail.

And when you step over the boundaries of my heart,
And test my faith in your words when we are apart.
You hurt her too, that little girl,
The one that couldn't speak..

She is the most important thing in the world to me,
And I profoundly protect her innocent and
pure fragility.

So please listen carefully when I share with
you my boundaries.

My Head

I am able to delete you because my head is stronger than my heart.
So my head must intervene, must save me.
This is for me and the lessons my soul must learn.
My ego is prevailing, I must catch it before it over turns.
Though I am strong and steady. I become weak at night when my heart is heavy.
So to feed my higher self and to teach my young learner. I must take control before my heart strikes the burner.

Knowing

As soon as I feel our directions are lost in the crowd, you appear in front of me again

Winded with surprise I hunt for clarity in your baby blue eyes.

Something that says nothing,
Or something that says everything.
In hopes that one of them will settle the pit in my stomach.

The pit of knowing again that you exist constantly,
However hard I may try to drown you out in the crowd-deep down I know……

You're there…we're there… and all the feelings coming rushing there again too….

Dive

I want you to dive into
Me.

Have your fingertips penetrate
Beyond my skin.

Until my blood flow tangles
Around you.
And my heart beat beckons you
Deeper.
Swimming inside me until you understand
every inch of my dancing bones.
And our warmth
Combines.
Combusts and
Explodes.

Surrender

I miss you my love,
But I'm not sure that's enough.

To rest and feel each other's breath rise and fall.
Make breakfast and take in a day of nothing at all.
Entangle on the couch with a movie then head
upstairs and feel each other moving.

I surrender it.

Naked Words

Your ego hears my words and takes them to fill it's tank. But they are false fuel because their source isn't from a place of adoration or lack. I don't see myself as less than you, or my words of love as an added value I don't hold in myself to be true. Their source is the exact opposite. No soul not whole or secure would be vulnerable enough to communicate their love.

Only the strongest of women would dare undress you with words so inspired. A privilege, and timeless gift that's been dissolved in modern fire.

The Root

I know I shouldn't love you but I do.

What is it that draws me to you?
All the senses in the world can't understand.

So what is it that draws me to you?

It's not really about you.
It's my comfort zone.

I learnt from my youth, I have to be alone in my truth.
That's what attracts me to you.

Your love is there but never quite followed through.

I don't blame you.

I'm working on forgiving myself for not accepting my true value.
Because I shouldn't love you but I do

Warm

Warm like your hand on my face.
Warm like the blanket around my waist.
Warm like your eyes catching mine.
Warm when our bodies intertwine.

Warm is what I'm craving.
Warm is what I'm wanting.
Warm is what I'm welcoming.

Meet me in this space if warm is what you're offering.

Our World

I live in a world where our hearts are braver than our heads.
Where our love won't cease at our death.

Where your eyes start my morning, and our lips end our days.

Where we tangle in between the sheets.

Where we read together, walk together, laugh, but also find such comfort in the silence, quietly viewing life around us.

I live in a world with you, but not for you. With passions and respect and strength.

If I close my eyes I can almost see those baby blues, and that cheeky white smile that goes with them too.

My Prayer

My prayer is as old as time.
That I will be mine and he will be his,
And we will be divine.

Give me strength to love and fulfill myself,
Give him vulnerability to embrace pure love in this life.

May we teach and learn and listen and communicate so much so that we can touch others as well as ourselves.

I am grateful for the lessons,
I pray I am fearless and vulnerable while learning.
And I thank him for his teaching.

May we love freely but true.

I am vulnerable and scared and brave.
Acknowledge my work and intentions,
so we can grow and flourish from this moment.

Rhythms

Come to me she said.
Come and caress my hand,
and let the wind of your movement blow through my hair.
Guide us with love not authority,
til our mouths and ears synchronize,
And we can find rest and comfort in each
other's rhythms.

Love is the Best Part.

Love is the best part,
And we have that now.
We struggle to express it.
Still we feel it.
And it engulfs us.

We walk and breathe and move through it.
Be still and open.
But how do we calm and relax the heart with its
ever present beat, steady and unrelenting.
let go, letting go
because love is the best part.

Harvest Love

I am digging deep-
Anticipating you.

Getting into the earth of my heart-
To clean space.

Adding mulch to harvest from fertile ground a love
that will grow through the seasons,
years and beyond

I am digging deep-
Anticipating you.

Getting into the earth of my heart-
To clean space.

Adding mulch to harvest from fertile ground a love
that will grow through the seasons, years and beyond

A Letter

Love me gently for I am sensitive. Be patient with my trust as I test that you are steadfast.

My soul is honest, but when I lie instead, it's born from fear where I want trust to grow in its bed. So meet me with love and my honesty will flow, where there were doors, bridges will grow.

My walls may seem deceptive, but they are rooted in sorrow. Self defense mechanisms I am trying not to follow.

Take comfort in my acknowledgement of my weaknesses and fears.
And if you hear them, know you must be dear. For me to be truly vulnerable is the gift that transcends years.

Light

Paradise Found

I pulled in my oars, tired of the resistance- and
chilled out floating down.

Sun on my face, nature all around-
Drops of water touched my skin-
Alighting anticipation in my already ecstatic body.

I smiled, paradise found.

Freedom Flow

I can feel it now,
The edge of my skin talking with my heart.

"Lets go- lets rest- love him- say yes- say no- jump- pause- breathe- sing- dance- scream- run"

My blood runs free,
Connecting all my muscles and veins.

Somewhere along the way they stopped talking- or I stopped listening.

I can hear you now, I can feel you now.

Freedom flow reigns again.

Divinity in Peace

There is divinity in peace.
A regal-ness in grounding.

With your soul planted and mind clear,
You exude confidence in your own space.

It is an egoless crown, not seen but adorn
throughout you.

An energy created from clearing, heart opening,
unconditional lightness-
of your timeless soul in your present human state.

I Found My Feet

I found my feet,
My soul imprinted in the sand.

The earth hugged my toes.
Detoxed my bones,
And lightened my load.

I lightly tread this new found land.

I danced on its support as my heart laughed
and smiled.
As if it knew all along,
We would tread soul deep,
One day on this sand.

Bella

Bella you wake
Bella you shine
Bella you love
Bella you live
Bella you dream
Bella

She Moved

She moved like her bones felt the soul of the earth.
She moved like she knew every hurt.
She moved like her compassion was endlessly deep.
She moved like she was inviting you into your deep,
Like she was pulling you into the depths of her being.
That souls vulnerable place,
With such confidence her strength made you weak.

Weak to surrender to your feats, anything that made you waver or favor others over your divine flavor.
The kind of physical expression that infects everyone who witness' with love and beckons them to take part.

She moved like the earth, stars and hearts were built to charge her heart.

She moved.

Gratitude

So I take a moment.
To reflect and think about everything that has brought me here.
Cursing myself for not surrendering to you sooner.

And then the moment absorbs me. It sweeps around me and hugs me. The sea breeze petting my hair and the waves penetrate my pores.

I'm in the painting and the moment is magic. I am the luckiest girl in whole wide world, just sitting here.

I'm going to inject this into my soul and carry it with me everywhere I go.

Cocoon

I can feel when I need to cocoon.

Where I used to stretch myself- I go in now.

Home to my comforts-
Writing, reading, learning.

Deep stretches and warm meals.

Rain tapping on the windows and water surrounding me in the bath.

A safe place to rest and digest, until the world calls me back again.

Serenity

When you find moments of pure serenity in your life:
Close your eyes. Absorb the smells and sounds.
Open your eyes, capture the sights.

You can take yourself there.

During the week, before bed, in a moment of upset:
Close your eyes, see the sights, smell the smells, hear the sounds. Your body doesn't know the difference.

You can take yourself there.

Light

The light in me, is a reflection of the light in you. What you want is already yours if you feel it true. Start with your heart and work your way out, until your heart fire overflows and your light pours out.

www.ingramcontent.com/pod-product-compliance
Lightning Source LLC
Chambersburg PA
CBHW051843160426
43209CB00006B/1134